The Camel's Pedestal

Poems 2009–2017

BY ANNE TARDOS

POETRY:

The Camel's Pedestal
I Am You [first US edition]
NINE
The Celebration
Both Poems
I Am You [first UK edition]
The Dik-dik's Solitude: New & Selected Works
A Noisy Nightingale Understands the Tiger's Camouflage Totally
Mayg-shem Fish
Cat Licked the Garlic
Uxudo

BROADSIDES:

Nine 31, 32, and *33, Woodland Pattern*
Ami Minden, Davis Museum, Literary Series, Wellesley College
Boomerang Suntan, University of Maine, Orono
I Was Brainwashed as a Child, There Was No Other Way, FluxFax Portfolio

WORKS EDITED WITH INTRODUCTIONS:

The Complete Light Poems, by Jackson Mac Low (co-edited with Michael O'Driscoll)
154 Forties, by Jackson Mac Low
Thing of Beauty: New and Selected Works, by Jackson Mac Low

RADIO AND MULTIMEDIA PERFORMANCE WORKS

Among Men, WDR Production; MoMA exhibit, and numerous live performances.

Apple Eaters, Multichannel video installation. Stefanotty Gallery, The Kitchen, Electronic Arts Intermix, and numerous live performances.

THE CAMEL'S PEDESTAL

POEMS 2009–2017

ANNE TARDOS

BLAZEVOX[BOOKS]
Buffalo, New York

The Camel's Pedestal, Poems 2009–2017
by Anne Tardos
Copyright © 2017
Published by BlazeVOX [books]

All rights reserved. No part of this book may be reproduced without
the publisher's written permission, except for brief quotations in reviews.

Printed in the United States of America

Design and typesetting by Geoffrey Gatza
Cover art by Anne Tardos

First Edition
ISBN: 978-1-60964-295-2
Library of Congress Control Number: 2017943764

BlazeVOX [books]
131 Euclid Ave
Kenmore, NY 14217
editor@blazevox.org

BlazeVOX

Acknowledgments

The Camel's Pedestal was edited in collaboration with Michael Byron. His dedication and hard work selecting the poems herein, and completing the book, were nothing short of vital. I feel extremely fortunate to be the recipient of his literary and editorial expertise, relentless work ethic, and sharp focus. Byron is a brilliant composer, and the last five poems in this book were written especially for him to be set to music for voice and chamber ensemble.

I thank Stu Watson and Robert C.L. Crawford, editors of *Prelude #2*, for publishing some of these poems. That issue of *Prelude* also included a thoughtful essay on my work by Stu Watson. My thanks to Ariel Resnikoff and Orchid Tierney, editors of *Supplement*, for publishing some of these poems; to Kurt Devrese, editor of the online magazine alligatorzine.com, for publishing "Gentle Deer on 10th Avenue," and "It Changes"; Daniel Y. Harris, editor of x-peri.blogspot.com for publishing "The Enigma of Being Jewish"; Dominique Lévy for commissioning the poem "GEGO" for the exhibition catalog *Gego: Autobiography of a Line*; Sylvia Gorelick, editor of the anthology *Symmetries: Three Years of Art and Poetry at Dominique Lévy*; Thomas Buckner for commissioning the song cycle "The Pure of Heart," "Philomel's Song," "Beginningless," "One," and "Tenderness in Late Afternoon Light." My deep gratitude to Geoffrey Gatza of BlazeVox Books for his excellent work and continued support over the years.

THE CAMEL'S PEDESTAL

I

THE ENIGMA OF BEING JEWISH

One throws one's trembling body forward.
Using gestures, one inscribes what one is saying.

Gender neutral, one is free to speak the unspeakable.

One doesn't speak.

Secretly, deep down inside, one finds the courage to plunge into the
    arena of contradiction, where pleasure and reality embrace.

One joins the fight against injustice and poverty—as one must.

We count as far as we can count, yearning for infinity, eternity.

We deliver the mail, grow orchids, grow weary, grow old, keep track of history, consider space-time to be a substance rather than a direction.

We contemplate time-reversal invariants, such as the shattered glass cinematically reassembling itself, landing on the table intact—the impossibility of which is somehow related to thermodynamics.

We find things to say, we clarify, codify and spotify, we establish a discourse, we break up, we destroy, we foresee the unforeseeable, we come to our senses.

We are amazed, we search for knowledge, we prolong, we hang on to pleasures, we are afraid, we feel strange desires stirring inside us, we make trouble.

We produce texts. Think about what to write. We implement and follow diversity policies.

What more can I say?

We are moved by childlike innocence.

Never mind the titles. They can be anything you like.
Bernadette once offered a long, witty list of possible titles.

A list.

A title.

A sheet of paper.

Clarice said that living doesn't take courage, but *knowing* that one
is living, does.

I often wonder how this is true.

I am standing in front of the closed doors of the future.

I am the outsider.

Forever forbidden.

The future is spreading through my limbs.

I overflow.

I am ashamed. I am afraid.

I tremble, I redden, I bleed.

The more I am afraid, the more I am hunted.

I'd be crazy not to go crazy.

5

Making small gestures, leaving traces.

Thrown into language, the Algerian Jew discovers that writing
    takes physical effort.

Could be Derrida, could be Cixous.

Not interchangeable, but like-minded.
Not substitutable, but compatible.
Not alike, but attuned.

The sunshine of Oran.
The French context.
The German family.

Displaced dispersed exiled.

It must be crisp not cryptic, if you want to write.

There is this come-and-go of ideas, impressions, fears, uncertainties.

Let them.

A rope.

      Any rope.

           Naropa.

Hold on to it and then let go.

Grab it when it comes around the next time.

Strange, friendly solitude.

An atypical Jewish girl from France, but not just that.

Make your own peace.   Invent it.

On this trip, we walk among the insects, we walk alongside them.

           They like it.

2

As the captain of this ship I am on, I keep a log.
The ocean is peaceful, pollution almost unnoticeable.

The dolphins.
	They follow me around.

Of course there is too much liking and disliking.

As the days wind down, underlined by the peculiar sound of the
cicada, a distant plaintive howl of unidentifiable origin is heard.
This is the country.

Living in multiple worlds simultaneously.
Each one is equally true.

The perfect blue sky behind the green trees make a
generous gesture.

Things can take a while. What things?

The approximation of what's on one's mind, a certain yearning for an
exact representation of thought, followed by an abandonment of the
illusion of ever being able to properly communicate one's thoughts.

Noon sun. I sit in the shade. A fragrant breeze comes along, a bird
makes itself heard. Nearly silenced by all this natural perfection.
But no, I keep writing.

Someone has to give permission.

I give permission.

4

Creamy thought-bubble ideal creamy super dreamy

Yeah, I really don't care what they think

It had to come to this
        It came to this
            It came that I couldn't any longer give much
        thought to opinions

It comes to caring. It comes.

Company. Rushed. Amass. Enjoy. Feel good. Doctor. Evansville.
It's one thing to say the word hummingbird, it's another to see one.

Off the books. Off-board. Finicky youthfulness. A cat. A bird.
A good look. Take one.

Appropriation. Vandalism. Senegal. Finally taking a stand.

Listening in. Participating. Border delineation. Tenderness.
Writing stuff.

Insect variations. The Insect Variations!

6

Inquisitiveness in aid of navigation.

The sun has something to say.   The future is being questioned.

      The past is baked in. Most of it.

Stepping up.

Is it lunchtime already?

The garden and the gardeners.
Bending over as a matter of immersion.

Ghostly communications. Apparent realities.
    And now.
Leave each other alone. Respectful harmlessness. No need to discuss.
Waiting.

For the lawnmower to stop.

My contributions. Behavioral art. Ridiculous mirrors. Cissexism.
Voilà. A branch just snapped. Where are the gentle deer?
On 10th avenue? How come?

So that feeling-of-being-watched thing.   Tackle that.

Broken concentration creates idea shards.   Tackle that.

She is his shadow. He is her shadow. Their dog is theirs.

Taking out the trash as a territorial statement.

How much wood would a woodchuck chuck if a woodchuck could chuck wood? As much as he could.

How long does a poem need to be?

This is not known.

Where am I supposed to turn?

Is it true that you must write each word as if it was your last?

I see many paths to a better life, many routines to engage in, voices to listen to, admired ones to imitate, parks to visit, animals to comfort, words to invent, phrases to think of, lives to improve, routines to follow, friends to invite over, temptations to resist, sounds to get used to or annoyed at—there is no shortage of things to do on the path to a better life.

9

Here is section number nine. Now what?

Mired in Africa, mired in India, mired in Chenshtochau.

My mother had Vienna carved into her soul, though she spent many
years in France, as a member of the Resistance, where she met my
Hungarian father, and where they decided to have me.
I was born into the Resistance.

To this day…

Is resistance the stuff of life? Forward motion defying resistance?

Resistance is easily explained in scientific terms. Philosophical terms.
Poetic terms.

Moving away from something means refusing it, rejecting it,
leaving it behind.

Clinging to childhood could be seen as a form of resisting resistance.

Death is the one to resist, until it isn't.

Coming of age.

Complaining.

Thinking about thinking.

Reliving life.

Poverty is humiliating. Poetry can also be humiliating unless it's uplifting.

The shame of imagined failure.

Disappointment.

Missed opportunities.

Thermal baths.

Tool sheds.

Mere interference.

Numbered sections of what poem. Defining the work before engaging in it, and after it's done. A definition of intent and content to invent.

Cixous: "[Rembrandt] paints the foreigner, the stranger in me, in you.

"The times when under the letter's sway we suddenly become the stranger, the foreigner in ourselves. We separate ourselves from ourselves. We lose ourselves. From sight, also."

What's going on here? Who is talking and to whom?

I say too much, I say too little.

Summery delirium.

We will see how it all ends.

Is this a stream of unconsciousness?

Can we dislodge the obstacles?

I reach back into the distant past, where I once lived by images.
Past, present and future give me different dynamisms.
Without them I would be a dispersed non-being.
 Memories are motionless, fixed in space.
Here, space is everything.
Within the being, the being of within, I feel at home.

All the spaces of past moments, the spaces where solitude was experienced, were places to rest.

Solitude allows one to work hard.

A bear bears the mark of sincerity.
She makes her own precarious shell as smooth and soft as possible.
The bear inhabits herself, and relies on the paradox of sensibility.
Her confidence in the world is key.

Surrounded by an atmosphere of happiness, the bear participates
in the mystery of form-giving life.

Enduring interest begins with the original amazement
of the naïve bear.

A strange sort of withdrawal.

One wouldn't be so bold as to presume to be included, unless
firmly invited.

Bachelard speaks of a house that turns out to be so beautiful, so
deeply beautiful, that it would be a sacrilege to even dream of
living in it.

(A Very Short Story)

He was giving birth to groups of words that were living
inside him as things.

End

It Changes

The flesh is sad, alas, and I've read all the books.--Mallarmé

The concept of an "invaded authorship," a writing influenced by
others, points to the unconscious of a text.

The strangeness of forever being here and elsewhere: Ever here
as elsewhere: Elsewhere as here.

I and the other: I as the other—Cixous

Foggy, incommunicable truth, where sometimes nothing is less true
than the truth.

What is it that makes me live so well and so badly?

It is my own self that I am painting.

Flexible and fluid as life itself.

The question is: Where do I place myself, where do I go?

I see everything and I see nothing at all.

As in physics, where matter cannot exist without interaction.

Can life exist without perturbation or agitation and unease?

Science speaks of perturbation theory, in which, for example, when
two fermions engage in interaction with bosons: that exchange
will have altered both fermions.

And the Buddha said "it changes."

It was dark then, ten minutes to eleven, the sky covered all over
with stars.

The following Sunday, it had been raining too heavily
to stroll around.

The next morning was just as gray as the last had been.

Some of those who steal things, steal love, psychiatrists say: those who
have inside their lives an empty space, need to fill it with love, if
they can, and they need to please others in order that others may
give them love.

Then they call each other darling more often than could be sincere.

Everything is literal.

What time is the train? I don't know: if we go to the station, a train will
    come—they always do.

I don't have anything special to do, so I turn the corner.
I know so many other places.
I was doing fine, I thought.
I was standing there, very still, across the street, a number of
    years ago—a newcomer, a stranger.

An old armchair in an old abandoned town, a faded sign that reads
    "coming," an old friendship that lasts a lifetime, coffee, the smell of
    decay, an oceanic experience, unity with all things, no holding
    back, snowcapped mountains, dark situations, suspense, and far
    away green forests marked on a map.

Continuing on the path of what could be but is not yet.

The present as passing, or rather as having passed.

Friendly faces sparkling water skin graft.

Sparkling water effervescence glittery nemesis cable.

Glittery, sparkling, never-ending life-span, keeping it clean.

Sparkling water, barking dogs, sparkling water, far-gone heat source,
    escalating honesty.

Barking elephant, barking water, an elegant element deeply calming.

Tranquility water deeply warming suddenly warning.
Waning taming tanning disappearing waving back, waving at me.

Buggy opposition water-stain; imagine a structure in front of you,
composed of all you've ever seen, heard, or otherwise experienced, I
mean the enormity of the accumulation . . .

All the sparkling details representing the complete totality of
cumulative elements of a human life and the sum of unrelated
experiences.

Watch the glittery water drizzle down Lizzie's neck, her hips and toes.

Our interconnectedness, unification, seamlessly interrelated here, and
   all the computers, and the forging of mass awareness, all of us
   knowing everything.

Baby doctor filibuster, quarreling is human.

   Yet truth is false, it's divided.

Division between inside and outside, where you cannot decide
   which is which.

I was trying to go inside the world, the garden, inside others—
I was outside.

I was young enough. It was not easy to be young enough.

The unity of the self, obviously an abstract concept.

Born many times through many ancestors, so I never know where
    I was born, there or here, then or now.

Memory as an intangible treasure creates the fragile ground
    we walk on.

I am a book—I have been written, and I am reading.

    If you lose somebody who is it, it's yourself.

Emotions are the result of fleeting familiarizations with new
    ways of thinking.

The new poem cannot be really new, yet its newness is
    what we strive for, and ultimately imagine.

It was a sultry August day, the earth was invaded by lifeforms from
    another planet.

It took some time for the whole strange image to sink in: a species not
    indigenous to earth, and I tremble remembering it even now,
    vague chills assail me as I try to picture their *eyes.*

Softly hissing at her reptile companion, Peyote, the mouse, as she was
    called, took a nap curled up in the little nest she had built for
    herself.

Who is this mouse, and who is this reptile companion, and shouldn't I
    relate, at least to myself, who I am?

I could also ask myself who will I be tomorrow, which would depend
    on what is happening now.

The internal storm that leaves me in search of any old port.

Constant refusal, denial, what am I searching for, what do I want?

What needs to be done will be done: time is never wasted.

Sales at Christmas capital bonus sales at capital fog.

Physical therapy post-op ritual, skinny foggy purchase capitalized.
Ritual bone break capital capital capital capital after shave.

Reaching the end of time, the bend of time.

Nothing is forbidden, nothing's allowed, authority nothing and
    nowhere to be found.

Projected reflection standpoint and echo are necessarily divided.
Division and beauty clash in the face of congruence.

You can't tell me what to do because I can't hear you.

This is where the break occurs.

The illusory sense of belonging—you can't really belong to
even a particular moment, since you and the moment pass
as soon as formulated.

No future and no past, only instants ticking through
an infinite present.

We float in space and space floats inside us.

This is where the dictionary comes in.

Nine toddlers dawdle down the River Nile, in their rowboat filled
with Siamese cats, amulets, scarabs, burial figures for the dead,
these little toddlers sitting among their Ptolemaic coins, mummy
wrappings, papyrus scrolls, and small glazed faience statues of
Thoth, the ibis-headed moon god, the god of wisdom, justice
and writing, patron of the sciences, and messenger of the sun god
Ra—gently down the river the toddlers row.

        Ra

Just then the black cat appeared on the roof, he crouched while
    I bribed him to love me.

The little beast did not want to be loved.

Cooking is passion. Bloom walks around Dublin with kidneys
in his pockets.

Safe and relaxed like a stone.

Give me the trusting mind: No doubts or delusions.

Let me mingle perfection with non-perfection.

Meaning and meaninglessness: the effort to differentiate fills me with
a certain sense of obligation.

Mutilated languages, ways to fix them, ways to repair.

The dualistic state I am in, static and stalling and idle, prevents all
possible progress.

What I need is a point of departure—any point, any departure.

Begin somewhere, no need to wait, just begin anywhere.

I begin by remembering the smell of the ocean and relive the sense of
being full of hope.

I'm ready and willing to play below my dignity.

I could be the mountain, the earth, the sky, or a little toad, or a little
    mouse, or the tip of its tiny nose.

My own death, the one I'm so afraid of: Imagining specific scenarios.
Restless anxious envious confused orphaned fearing frightful
    loneliness during such a transition.

The ways of seduction, suction, and abduction, the excitement at
    being rescued.

Silence, fundamental quietness, the result of thought.
Unanswerable metaphysical questions as the intellect expands into
    language.

The ultimate nature of all things, the true state of things expressed in
    phenomena but inexpressible in language.

Futility generators generously fuming, vaping on the sidewalk while
    others describe suchness and the nature of all things.

Letting things be.

2

Dorothy's little bed another corner, from which a ladder in its path.
Timidly up to the door, how are we to get away, or next day, maybe.
Patiently reading a book is where they entangled again. Out of a long
conversation: stick to the task.

The reader understands the magnitude of the enveloping story.
A child's vision in contact with mythical forces, departure times,
melancholy caterpillars.
We need some elephants shIny ones.
I don't care a great deal never mind louder.
Silence in a moment more people in the garden.

Oh, of course, that sounds amazing. Under the leaves, just like me.
Nothing, she said nothing, I think I will go and meet her. No more
insects while walking in the opposite direction. What kinds of insects,
very large ones that talk.
A goat in white so young and gentle so unsuspecting—with luggage.

A gnat, as if nothing bad has ever happened.
An agony of haste, crawling branch above your head. And now who
am I and what exactly do I call myself?

She was enjoying her lunch.

Falling into the luxury of moral collapse, she was anything but gentle.

The instinctive complicity of thin legs and tangled hair, a plan to live as long as crystal drops.

I see no pattern here. Pitter patter agriculture level best another job.

I stay safely within myself, a place I know as home, merely to breathe, sipping hot spicy wine.

Human curiosity is of two minds, bound to sympathize, living with philosophy within the limitations of one's time in the world.

Dinner parties unfold into soft shimmer of human pleasures.
Warm soothing mist, it was real, it had happened, it was hers.
Looking for relief from herself, she reached into the farthest
deepest darkest most suppressed reaches of her being.

She located the place of moral insights and principles.

Tiptoeing around the good and the terrible, she found her
inner process to be in need of outer criteria.

A bird's screech overhead is taken as a signal for the next step.

Cultivating patience with all her heart, she didn't understand
what was happening.

This shapeless nameless endless human anguish.

Derailed vigilantism ectoblastic wannabe linseed oil.

Skin condition, on a good day, neural tube Mallarmé.

Drum beat eloquence decomposing blueberry invention.

Elegant predicament quantum river digitized family.

Breeze management, funny movies, arms, hammers.

Normal syntax anxiety, funky meditation technique.

Mimesis of modernity. Scintillating paradoxical textuality.

All of this is irrevocably amazing.

Sentence frenzy counting words and hyphens.

Many thoughts and observations will have been noted here.

Long ago picture, resembling the Bay.

There is a variety of contractile elements in the scheme of life.

Contractility of the heart, for example.

Tokyo Subway

I've no time to write that I have no time to write.

Pleasure in rhythm, finality fulfilment, triangular postings.
Tokyo subway.

Furthermore humidor nevermore sycamore troubadour herbivore.

Recipe precipice, calculating options, impressive instabilities,
mind body conflict.

Athletic psychology, country of amnesia, libidinal artifact,
lemon-lime handicap.

Calibrating unsettled kittens, changing landscapes, tiny insects
quietly working.

Did somebody knock on the door? Do words work as wood works?

Universal granite, life on this planet, terrible and hard, with a few
crumbs thrown in.

Dangerous opinions, self-destructive gestures, wish to be on good
terms, antiquated skin.

Longing and uncertainty in the face of another lump of mortal procreation.

Thankful for my attention being diverted, besieged and attacked from all sides, finding a good place to start.

Like a hummingbird I taste the nectar sipping sunshine.

Movements of language as the intermediary between the conscious and the unconscious.

The nobility of greatness. The radical avant garde.

It's like a composition, you see, one that contains related and obliquely related material.

The thread weaving from experience to experience is invisible to me.

And there is nothing really blue in this representation.

Sunlight faintly green, golden in sea and sky.

From one moment to another moment in time, moving in direction-independent ways, abandoning the notion of an absolute "now," denying the reality of the future.

It is necessary that I exist or I would not be able to make this very statement.

It is possible that a cat and a dog meet and go for a walk, and it is also possible that a cat and a duck take a walk together.

It is obligatory that we keep a certain order in this madhouse.

It is permitted that I drink an occasional glass of wine, but it is obligatory that I drink water every day.

It is forbidden that I harm myself or others.

It has always been the case that anything alive strove to remain alive, it couldn't help itself.

It was the case that earlier today I came across modal logic; formalized philosophical notions of possibility and necessity, with the above propositional predicates.

Is a necessary proposition necessarily necessary?

. . . about to burn out, expire complicatedly, give or take a trillion years.

Is there ever a quiet place, where matter can rest, in a serene and well-lit place where stuff can breathe and sit in peace?

Such a state may be hard to imagine for those whose existence is rooted in contradiction, varying degrees of stress, exactingness.

I'm looking for a place where there are no needs, no urges, no life as we understand it.

No titillation of experiencing true chaos, and endless series of problems to solve and resolve.

Such a place would not really be of any use to us.

Such a place could not exist.

This is the point from which to push off.

Carefully listening to the appearance of an acceptable notion.

My fractured reasoning, inward dialogue, tripping on a stair
that isn't there.

I am lost in a desert of my own making.

Pico de la Mirandola and the dignity of humans.

Conditions tend to be favorable.

We want our privacy, space, identity, we want our teeth, hair, and all
our vital organs. We want a massage.

A familiar text, written a few billion years ago, I mean, how could I
possibly remember, when space-time measurement and
multiverse poetry were visibly detached, so that weakness was
avoided, toyed with, accepted.

Certain knowledge must remain out of bounds, we couldn't handle
the information, in the way a grasshopper would have trouble with
hermeneutics, or a marmoset with the deep structure of
the cosmos.

By attempting to introduce fresh air into my mind, I only muddy the
waters, making one thing clear: the more I seek clarity the more it
eludes me, wears me down in the vain attempt to achieve the
unachievable—ideas that get past my censorious nature and
exacting mind, occasionally allowed into the text, slipping past
my disapproval and doubt.

I recognize this.

Humans

Humans wish to be quiet and happy, each in their own way.

Nothingness is to be *experienced* instead of merely considered.

Negative events, troublesome bacteria, sorrow and indignation
and what about the artist?

Adagio sostenuto under the moonlight, do it once more,
solar panel dictation.

I feel I have the right to rummage through all that I see and hear.

Solo piano, sparsely notated for a few feathery friends dozily, virtually sing song matinee, oozing reality out of each rivulet, while others look on and listen carefully.

Wherever you go there will be anguish, as you listen to the missing persons and their mysterious disappearances.

The image cannot be projected or effectively treated by anyone in the vicinity of reflection.

Copious bellicose fruit punch division, at long last, and the very least.

Gender balanced original demands of unknown children and their children and theirs.

Good-morning optimism every day without fail.

Today I understood that everything is about something else.

Mania assumes the shape of unanswerable riddles, softening, just
now.

I try to reconcile myself with no income at all, you must try it
sometime.

Pastime party with a flourish, knife and fork, implied kinship.

The born outsiders, the unwanted, yearning for disappointment,
listening but not seeing.

On the edge of things forever sleeping in soft animal ease.

He could see no sign of humanity in her, yet there it was
but only as a last resort.

Facing the perpetual problem of catastrophes; broken arms, legs,
heads, maybe even necks.

Repetition Sunday, pillow lost my keys, missed trains, forgotten
appointments, not in the least happy.

The whole thing is clear. The brick wall, the white paint, the office
chair, the big moment, the high, the pleasure, the relief—all clear.
Seeking pleasure is clear, and calling all of it clear is also clear.

Let's see now: Carbon copy. Dulcimer. Ropes around my mouth and
rosemary-flavored lollipops. Decameron and the Black and the
Blue. The camera and suddenly Sisyphus, then the Classics, the
translation and its consequences.

Drizzle the bucket of frozen rope.

The cognitive value of happiness and well-being function as endless
enjoyment.

Collective enjoyment's responsibility endlessly benevolent folly.

Farcical solemnity and monkeyish ridicule, not a fool, but a woman of
the world.

In frustration of this natural authority, they chose to speak on behalf
of the ill mannered.

Deviations from daily routine—a threat to established rules.

This is not a movie or a novella, what did you expect?

You need to understand what this is: they will barely let you say half a
sentence before losing patience with you, so this is not a movie.

Carefully crafted pathways lead to unknown places where longing
leaves hesitation behind.

On A Limb

Primal brightness on a hot afternoon
When grass is loud with insects
It is summer

Without collapsing completely
I hold on to a benign instant

We are divided creatures
in an interactive world
we move steadily
in a continuum

I will find a way
    The sky may grow darker
        But I will find a way

Each day is like an entire life
Encapsulated miniature of the bigger event we call life
Sameness on a different scale

You know what the world is like—in theory.

I live the lives of those I encounter, and they live mine.

My thoughts reflected in your thoughts, on your screen.

Our unique social dimension coupled with our scientific imagination.

Together we walk and feel the collective path laid out before us.

I ask myself: Where am I going with this?

Where people greet one another by touching the ground with their
    forefinger and then raising it to heaven?

Where they struggle with their inability to textualize the world
    around them?

Finding the exact place where language and reality intersect?

Where they lose faith in their own talent or in the larger possibilities
    of literature? Is that where I'm headed?

My hair is growing faster than my self-awareness.

Fearful habitat, misconception rickshaw, levelheaded apprehension, never known to flinch.

Ferris wheel calamity, tennis courts and subways, Lower East-Side kitchenette, ordinary freak.

Big dog nemesis, vigilant and skilled, namby-pamby naked kitty, narcoleptic squid.

Factory worship, democratic dolphin, existential deficit, harpsichord and fish.

Crisscross centipede, knowledgeable inchworm, apprehensive buffalo, unexpected cyst.

Corkscrew tenderness, liberating vapors, slightly damaged apple cart, many ways to kill.

Jigsaw leverage, Lower East Side kitchenette, kettle brewing lustily, many drops to spill.

Banjo sentiment, unobtrusive labels, level-headed apprehension, not a drop to drip.

Morse code residence, charismatic lassitude, populated tenement, laminated zinc.

Complicated turnaround, misconception rickshaw, emasculated madrigal, apricot and dish.

Ferris wheel calamity, tennis courts and subways, pantomiming habitat, other people's ticks.

Flip-flop medicine, infantile arrangement, sentimental elephant, kindergarten shtick.

First-class surgery, dilapidated farmhouse, genderbending trivia, never-ending blip.

Day-job etiquette, application moisture, seven little elephants in a tiny little sink.

Innate elegance, preference for timber, information exercise, energetic lynx.

A slightly elevated temperature and a quiver of conscience.

Categorized mango, ordinary safety-pin, deep-thinker's daydream,
never having been.

Monkey nickel bucket panic, cantilever elbow, instrumental step
ladder, lemon yellow zest.

Apparatus recognition, confidential nature, never ending snowfall,
Nagasaki junk.

Funny little time-lapse, language being sculpted, frozen airport
traveler, complicated shirt.

Rice-bowl equivalent, catastrophic blunder, irritating spicy dinner,
Vichy water's wish.

Hideous mountain range, identity avalanche, fun-loving Kodiak—not
even in jest.

Guinea-pig excellence, voluntary whisper, diagnosed as perilous,
dangerously slick.

Melancholy Lizard

A buzzard in a blizzard, not like the old days at all.

Motionless gentleman occupant forger, visible ginger, pelican's posture.

Transitory ephemera, particulate positron, Rockaway mockery, dedicated chintz.

Digital wizardry, miserable lizard, second-time enclosure, fenugreek and dill.

Notebook devastation, incremental body language, modest ideas, to name just a few.

Emblematic Winnebago, complex machinery—don't hurt my feelings.

Way to go criminal, marginal questions, accommodating girlfriend.

Historical engagement, sympathetic affidavit, marriage penetration.

Echinacea sitzbath, frivolous lawsuit, flocks of birds on rocks.

Mogadishu hothouse, Sichuan sunshine, cumbersome cummerbund.

I should say something that everyone can immediately understand.

Can a person not narrate and still be happy?

Instinctively everyone lived for food, blushing with coy intimacy.
It's not unusual.

All art is based firmly on mathematics both in the sea and in the air.

An anthology and an ant walk into a bar.
An aardvark joins them, offering them each a joint.

An embryo listens intently to music emanating from somewhere.

An earthshaking event shakes the globe.

For ever and ever can't be, for there is no forever, or rather there is
only forever, which means that there is only now.

Nor would I like to experiment with this sentiment.
Nor is he always as handsome as he does.
Neither an ear nor a question would I touch.

By the time you read this, I will be located elsewhere, like a
distant galaxy.

Turned the void into vivid, the city into silly, the spotless pavement
   into a camel's pedestal, found venom in thunder, located humor,
   fingered an image, labeled a tuna, saw dragon in marriage,
   nurtured a guilty spider and petted a tiny tiger.

That's been my day so far.

Meanwhile people are killed in distant locations, tensions run
   high in Odessa.

Three people in Burundi on Friday.

Urban community gun research close to finding chilling effects.

Children, little cats, tiny little mice, innocent little lives.

We will urgently need that water.

Quality-of-life improvements on a grand scale, not to be confused
    with election-year issues.

Collapsing irrigation by agricultural warfare, taking on the water
    lobby. Seeking out information, finding a balance.

Concepts remain static pictures of an essentially dynamic reality,
    while the right-wing assault on women turns into a sick debate.

And there she went, exploring her consciousness, and all the unease
    and malcontentment, forcing her to limit her activities to a few
    unnamed and unspoken tasks she would rather not discuss, for
    fear of being interrupted, or worse, scrutinized.

Stepping into the river: The point and pointlessness of pointing.

The old *Salon of Tenderness*, where the specialty of the house is always
    the same: You are there already.

Jenny Benny and their money, Hollywood and Sunset Shazzam.

Depraved-heart murder by six officers, their grossly reckless injury, their depraved indifference, depraved-heart callousness toward the prisoner.

False imprisonment combined with a rough ride, suspect intimidation.

Recklessness and carelessness amounting to a level of negligence sufficient to serve as evidence of criminally culpable intent.

Rough ride inside a depraved heart.

Dismay disbelief opposition dismay dissent disbelief opposition
opposition opposition

Dissent opposition rage dissent rage fury dissent opposition
opposition

Dissent dissent rage dissent disbelief rage difficulty breathing rage

Opposition rage dissent rage dissent rage dissent rage dissent

Rebellion resistance resistance resistance difficulty breathing
resistance resistance dissent

Rage dissent fury rage fury fury fury fury fury

Difficulty breathing rage rage disbelief rage fury rage wrath

Anger wrath wrath anger anger anger anger anger anger

Dissent opposition disbelief dissent dissent dissent dissent dissent
dissent!

Ignorant immature headstrong incurious uninformed self-important
    puffed up arrogant
Repulsive dishonest deceitful corrupt offensive ill-mannered ghastly
    vile insane
Irresponsible, denying reality, vulgar uncontrolled raging flailing
    thrashing beating
Despicable revolting contemptible disgraceful loathsome nasty
    disgusting appalling sickening
Unreliable devious unpredictable erratic vain hopeless ineffective
    traitorous dangerous
Useless at best, deadly at worst, depraved debauched bad
Noxious deleterious pigheaded undeveloped inflexible stubborn
    toxic injurious criminal
Oblivious to the real world, unknowing, insensitive obtuse detestable
Blasé, and any other adjective you care to ascribe

3

At the Movies

You remember Kitty. Yes, I had to let her go, she was a nice enough
　　lady, but drowned?
Let's hope the perpetrator is caught and punished with the full force
　　of the law.
Assuming the time of death would have been after your arrival,
　　whoever killed her would still be here.
Love the twisty part—a gorgeous shade of brown.
The slither of a satin skirt.
She is not violent, she's French.
Lovely building, bay window, tall ceiling.
Perhaps something more glamorous perhaps some satin or silk.
Not too showy: a woman must know her style.
I don't believe he killed his wife, but he left town, and we don't know.
I am sure that we'll get to the bottom of all this.
Well, I think this calls for some nocturnal investigation.
Sit down and I will pour you some cocoa.
I was extremely agile, guilty of breaking into the salon, I'm happy to
　　pay for the fabric, luckily it's my style.
Note that the head wound from the iron wasn't lethal—the victim
　　was smothered to death in a bowl of beads.
You think I'd kill someone over a string of pearls?
Whoever we're looking for, it's time they met their match—have I
　　ever shown you my Columbian emeralds?
Un peu d'silence s'il vous plait! Why exactly are you here, Miss?

She is here to help me recover my hat.

Anyone taking things into their own hands will be arrested and
charged.

If it was a rope that killed him, how did he come to be hanging by a
scarf?

People usually kill for love or money.

A suggestion is not the same as an order.

I'd like to see *you* manage my sewing machine.

He might be rich and handsome, but you know Gertie, she'd never let
anyone down.

Yet I hear that you and Gertie were close.

I didn't like Gertie but I didn't want to see her die!

You're right—I'm off my game.

Bruising on the neck, crushed windpipe.

Where is the gun that killed him? How was I to know?

The diamonds, ice, nice big bloke: Security guard let me in—
didn't think you'd mind.

How can I be of assistance—what's that? Jimmy's book? You're not in
it. That bothers me. He never mentions you.

Did they even tell you about the heist? You killed him with that gun.
He deserved it—he just left me there—went off and pulled the heist—
he took that from me—and years later, Jimmy writes a book and
you're not in it.

The more you read the more you realize you weren't even worth a
mention, so then I went looking for him, and then I found him: What
are you still doing here? Was this some kind of a joke? I asked him
why, you weren't smart and not hard like Billy.

I'll be the final chapter in *your* life, just go. They shut me out, I
watched him die.

Give me the gun, you've done it, you'll be famous, you're the man who
killed Jimmy the Gin, yeah, yeah, breaks my heart that he was killed
by one of his mates.

They romanticize their lives, each other, themselves, but reputation,
respect, doesn't mean anything if you can't look at yourself in the
mirror at the end of the day.

Hello, room service?

The babysitter walks home alone late. A sudden death.

There is one other matter: We found a bottle of digitalis—deadly
nightshade—quite lethal.

What do you mean she died?

This sudden death: The letter, the gun, the worries.

I don't think I was a very good wife: I don't think I ever loved him,
you see: When he proposed it just seemed impolite to refuse.

The Killings at Brighton Beach. I mean who'd want to bump off
an eighty year old spinster? It doesn't make sense.

Yes, a broken neck and a shooting—all in a day's work.

I must tell the bees. You see, you have to tell the bees when somebody
dies. Otherwise they just clear off.

4

GEGO

I

The accidental concurrence of a poetic and artistic thought.

Where lines intersect lives.

Where language intersects reality.

Where knots are tied to hold it all together.

All ~ *Alles* ~ *das All.*

All is subjected to the rules of the universe which contains all.

Quiet observers, we gaze at the world thoughtfully.

II

A line in a poem addresses a line in space.

Moved by the urgent desire to establish a structural system,
she creates a space where reason rules.

She keeps it clean.   Even cleaner.

She delights in making it.

Geometry and physics inspire purity of heart.

She draws a fine line between a fine line and a fine line.

III

The hand becomes the tool of a distant sphere.

Using lines to delineate, the artist's hand reaches into space and
comes up with a whole new space.

Strategic distribution of mass . . .

Vertical ground reaction forces . . .

Flexural stiffness . . .

Continuous fields let air and light into an open system, implying
infinity, demonstrating thoughtfulness.

Points in space-time become the joints—recurring points of departure.

IV

The artist enjoys this.

"Just doing."

Life is to be enjoyed, she says. If not, then why . . .

She works "by reason of making," yearning to extend what she
    already knows.

She doesn't know where it comes from.

Yet with each line she draws, she knows there are hundreds more
    waiting to be drawn.

She points to the charm of a line in space.

The humanity of a line—"line as human"—profound love for the
    human being.

You could say that the structure becomes a metaphor for a historically
    inflected life.

I use the words of the tribe to inscribe my singularity.

    The parrot-meter is running.   Ticking away.

We exist and we don't exist. It's up to us.

You see how life is.

Your suffering is behind you.

Kandinsky's struggle between tonalities, lost equilibrium principles

    falling apart, unexpected drumbeats, big questions, apparently

    aimless aspiration, apparently desperate urgency and longing,

    shattering the chains and attachments that make several things

    one, antagonism and contradiction.

The choppiness of communication

    The fragmentedness

The infinitely increasing distance between everything and

    everything else.

His life ended

      Whichever god he was

        Sang before the sea and lands

Think of the spheres as transparent and interpenetrating—not static

    shells but concentric ripples traveling simultaneously out from

    and in toward each center.

They are separated now.

One of them is gone and the other is extending the gesture of

their time together.

Their succor.

I am one possibility.

Reality is the contextualizing of random information, following

certain principles.

The pure of heart

I like to think

Fight back as long as possible.

Coming into being.
     Finding something to do.
        Occupying.

When I sing, it is of Philomel, the nightingale.
That cool nightingale, who understands the tiger's camouflage
   totally.

It's so quiet today—I don't know what to say.

The uncertainty of the uncertainty, and then the uncertainty.

Millions of ancestors inhabit me, arguing among themselves.
   I can barely hear myself think.

Afflictive emotions and dissonant mental states cloud the picture.

   Enmity sets in.
      Mistrust and disappointment.
        The discourse of error.

Resisting an appetite for destruction that takes hold of desire, in the
   final outcome of the struggle in which the two combatants face
   off, leaving them with no one to determine who won and who lost.

I symbolize who I am—as simple as that.

With great flexibility and good cheer, if a tad inexact, but determined, generous, and sophisticated; composed of foggy material that's solidifying with every day that passes, blindly staying afloat in some way, becoming human, with gusto and abandon, finally becoming invisible and, in spite of harrowing circumstances, against all odds, recognizing an image reminiscent of another reality, a means of transport into another world, as real as the one I'm trying to escape from, by entering this other existence.

A character in my play.
    Both bigger and smaller.
      The audience.
        Me too.

I live on the intersection where language and reality meet. Where the word "pepper" cannot make me sneeze.

Rupture
    division
      segregation-anxiety-dread
and the heebie-jeebies.

Distortion is all there is. Reality is continually being recreated by various other realities.

The inner child, the lazy lavender slumber in the pine forest, where need becomes desire, and where You are the celebration.

BEGINNINGLESS

Life is a raw event

I give you roses   You give me roses

As I speak and as you listen, I feel the traction of my words in the
   terrain of your mind
We speak of the great emptiness which is ultimately empty of itself

(It is not reality either)

We discuss the limits of thought
The paradox of expressibility

The familiar

    the habitual

       we appropriate

Our mental attitudes then crystallize into instincts

Detached observation of brilliant force fields
    Luminous displacements

The ride of a lifetime

    The buzz of electricity

        The comfort of oblivion

            Staring at the ocean

                Inhaling heady sea vapors

                    The fullness of time

An increasing sense of urgency

    Inexplicable in light of a conscious attempt at slowing down

As if deceleration itself suggested friction

        Who am I and what do I mean by who am I?

Hume

Human

Creative power of the mind amounts to no more than the faculty of

    compounding

        transposing

           augmenting

              or diminishing the materials afforded us

    by the senses and experience

The muddy particulars of experience continually give us new material
to digest assimilate reject or rearrange in different degrees

Like seaweed, we undulate

We discuss zero, a finite moment fixed within our infinity

We say our infinity as we would say our solar system or our galaxy

We sense that each instant covers the entire world

We know that life doesn't happen to us
We happen to it

And what we make of all this stuff is up to us
Our inventions tend to be arbitrary
Much is about restraint and mindfulness
courtesy
empathy
focus

Not to give in—not to succumb
Not to wallow not to slouch
Not to slip not to fall

I have nothing better to do than to be here now.

Delicate gene pool

      Glitter kindness

            Unexpected chemistry

Thought exists

      Rigid necessity

I surge forward, feeling an elastic exhilaration.

This is the current situation as it stands:

      Everyone I've ever been I am now

All kinds of inspirations and illuminations,

Points of clarity and rays of grace

I don't know a better point to start from.

Time is invariant.

It doesn't flow and it doesn't pass.

We pass.

We learn that we are dealing with images. It doesn't matter what the fantasy is, as long as we engage in a reality that's navigable.

We are in the best place at the best moment.

By protecting me, you protect yourself.

Fusion, symbiosis, reciprocity, unquestioning trust.

We wouldn't settle for less.

Humble enough to do the next thing.

The microtonal inflection of a bird, insatiable, atavistic.

The weirdness of being human.

The brain thinking about the brain ...

A sense of being.

No reason why Nirvana should be hidden from me.

The blowing out of the flame of the Self.

Look upon death as something hygienic.
Tenaciously, youthfully, deceptively, accidentally.

Who is to say how this will be understood.

Existence is assured to those who overcome every obstacle, and
    where evolutionary bonanza can cause *being* to overcome
    non-being; and where we can see cascading enzymes within
    a single cell of the brain.

It's laughter that makes life's music.

Genetically predisposed to rolling on the floor, slapping knee,
    doubling over, weeping with mirth. Enough stability to keep
    things from collapsing into total chaos.

The right tone, a disciplined mind, and you're good.

        Mine is the ever perpetuating fricassee of life's continuity.

On those genre-free nights, she just writes and writes.

TV's flickering series of trivial, momentary, unreflective,
   uncomprehended images. Lambent shadows of things,
   themselves copies of real things.

The capybaras, giant rodents, who are easily pushed around
   by swans, must also symbolize who they are.

Fuddy-duddy shame-face. What am I doing here?

Swim butter sway
         split-level reptile
                  Bombay doorway rickshaw.
                     All part of the puzzle.
                        Every bit of it.

Ambiguity and motivation, subject-object relationship, immediacy.

Attention to quantum physics, deluxe lingerie, silence, blood-work,
   interlocking dreams, happy thoughts, Eros, cats and dogs,
   a few half-truths.

Sun spots to fear. Moroccan lavender to sniff. Great works of
   literature. Big complicated images. Organic farming. The South
   Pole. Imagination, intellect, contradiction and conflict. The
   Mediterranean Sea. A full system scan, and the basic oneness
   of the universe.

Innocence picks up the shape of a word, waking up early, chilled.

A quiver of conscience, a sudden twinge of anxiety. Did I do the right thing? Did I make a mistake? The crowds within me are having lively discussions.

Negative events, troublesome bacteria, sorrow, indignation and
what about the artist?
The artist looks to mathematics both in the air and in the sea.
The process requires solitude, a contemplative atmosphere.
Peculiar conditions.

The right to rummage through all that I see and hear.

I see everything, I see nothing at all, yet it is myself that I am painting.

I follow carefully crafted pathways, leading to unknown places,
where longing leaves hesitation behind.

Resting on the edge of hills that lead to nowhere, forever sleeping in
soft animal ease, guided by the warm, soothing mist and the soft
shimmer of human pleasures.

Making it all up, imagining a function.

Ingeniously living within the limitations of one's time in the world.

If we accepted a reality beyond human understanding, a bird's song
    overhead could signal the next step to take.

The cognitive value of happiness, and well-being, offers endless
    enjoyment.
Collective enjoyment's endlessly benevolent folly.

Sticking to the task, understanding the magnitude of the story,
    mythical forces, departure times.

Tacit appreciation of life, experiencing each moment, each other, the
    fantasy of being, this constructed imaginary reality, applying all
    measurements conceivable, an enormous system of
    understanding, a network of people, plants, and animals.

A certain preparation of mind, where tenderness in late afternoon
    light sits at the edge of a chair.

Takes my breath away.

Anne Tardos, French-born American poet, is the author of ten books of poetry, and editor of three collections of poetry by Jackson Mac Low. Her work has been translated and published in dozens of anthologies and journals around the world. Tardos pioneered a unique multilingual writing style, often complementing her texts with video stills, photographs, and collages. Her writing is renowned for its fluid use of multiple languages and its innovative forms. She has worked in numerous media, creating performance pieces, radio plays, videos, and musical compositions.

Her multilingual and multimedia works have been presented at the Museum of Modern Art, New York; the West German Radio, WDR; the XLIV Venice Biennale; and in many international sound poetry festivals, including Festival La Bâtie, Geneva; text-ljud Festival, Stockholm; Scene Wien, Vienna; and Zwischentoene, Cologne.

Since moving to New York in 1966, she maintained lifelong friendships with artists Richard Lindner, Saul Steinberg, Sam Francis, Larry Rivers, Vito Acconci, Ay-O, John Cage, Judith Malina, Simone Forti, Nam June Paik, Charlotte Moorman, George Maciunas; art dealer Felix Landau, architects Vally and Serge Sabarsky; poets Jackson Mac Low (longtime partner and collaborator), Jerome Rothenberg, Lyn Hejinian, Anne Waldman, Robert Creeley, and other figures of the New York avant-garde.

A Fellow in Poetry from the New York Foundation for the Arts, Tardos lives in New York City with her husband, the composer Michael Byron.

Made in the USA
Monee, IL
07 July 2026

56550080R00062